SHELF

I0156716

RUFO
QUINTAVALLE

Sagging
Shorts

Set in Trump Mediaeval with LATEX.

ISBN: 978-1-952386-06-0 (paperback)
Library of Congress Control Number: 2020950717

Sagging Meniscus Press
Montclair, New Jersey
saggingmeniscus.com

Acknowledgments

Parts of this poem have been published in the following places: *Belleville Park Pages; Big Bridge; elimae; Enchanting Verses; Field; Retort Magazine; Shadowtrain; The Opiate*. The first 15 sections of this poem have been published by corrupt press as a bilingual chapbook with a facing French translation by Ian Monk.

Author's Note

This poem is a line-by-line rewrite of the 1882 version of
Walt Whitman's "Song of Myself" where I have kept the
first and last letter of every line and rewritten the middle.
From time to time other formal constraints are used as
well but hopefully the enjoyment of the poem is not de-
pendent on prior knowledge of these rules.

SHELF

1.

Itself,
An amiable
Follow thru

I'll
Impress

Matter
Both his and mine
Into a thin
Hopscotch

Carapace
Rewritten
Inside and refilled
Naturally

2.

Heady ideas
Interest
The theocrat

This will be less
It will start
Its meandering road
In me

There is so much—
Eyebrows, stubble
Manbreasts
The soft down
That joins balls and
Anus
The bristling
Thighs and calves
The belly and the bellybutton

Had enough? Hair enough?
Hair of the head
Hair of the naked toes

Shoes are for pussies
Yet
You wear shoes
You compromise
Yourself

3.

I know where it will end:
Bed

The creamy tallow
Numinous warm glow
A nervous swallow
Now

Undo me
Adamic word

Om. The ever convex
Apple

The ego

Submitting to its
Sensual
Id

Consensual

Like a man
Turned woman

Socrates' advice
Know yourself

Why damn
Not

It beats inching
Along the road
Led by
Some other guy's
Truth toward
A prethought
End

4.

The
Plan:
To know
More or less
The me
That sweats
Belches
Thinks my own
Belief

As if I am
Solitary
Like that
Little boat
Bobbing in the night

Bullshit. I is
In life, of it

5.

In it with you
And all the other

Loosely knit
Nameless seekers that
Oceanic sense

In uniting
Has made
At once consentient
And apart

Sexual mesh
A priceless boon
A way to turn
Away from others
And yet not be
Alone. Leaves
Above us as we dream
Allonged in a unified field

6.

And then there is this:
Handfuls of substrate
In the kitchen

Overhead, a raincloud
Accumulates like an argument
Bursts and is gone

Or it can happen

Otherwise, vatic
Announcements
Glide from the tongue
Kindle into fire

And eat themselves

The morning passes
Into noon
Imperceptibly, a calm
Intransigence is
All around us

Then it too passes
Day becomes afternoon
Darkness

On the grass
And over everything

If one could win
At this

What would one win?
At dawn

The breeze
The tiny death
And a fat
Ampersand

As
Answer

7.

Have you known
It in your heart?

If so, then what is
Around
The thing understood?

If there is enough
In the jars on the shelf
Then make me stew

Empty the
Flour into the saucepan
Find some lard
Four cloves
Fenugreek and peppercorns
Fry the onion

Uncork a red
Ingest with gusto
And leave it for a day

8.

There
In the intimacy overheard

There by the windowsill
In this cheap

Trim room
Is where I found heaven

There are places
That are forever
True to us
This
Tiled hotel
Teaches me still
To pay heed
To the city's various
Wavelengths;
Warm summer nights
Whispered decorum
Angry voices
In the court

9.

They
Turn
Toward
The stew

It is good
In winter
Its spicy
Aggregates

10.

All the hurt
We
Inflict
Knowingly, the
Failure

To understand
Mean-hearted talk

To those
In a fragile
Youthful place

It will
Haunt us like a nimbus
On a hospital bed
Sheet

They live
In peace
That look
Around them
And see that
All things
Are themselves
And of the mass;
Hunger and lunch
Is slave and master

11.

The nine
Twenty
Train gets in at five

Some refreshments in the park
Should weather allow

Walt
An old grubber

Will show you
Your room

Do remember
To tip him

The dollar
Looks less

And less
Itself these days

They say the man must swim
That used to catch
The ferry

12.

This part
Is thin

Banal;
Everyone

Fills
The blanks
Or else
Turns the page

13.

The gray-bearded man
Told me
He'd
Hired
This

Image
Impresario

I was planning
To sing
A song

Of generations
I needed to be

More
Than I seemed

I followed his
Advice
And now all
Acquiesce
And come
After me

14.

The lucent
Young men
That pledge
Fidelity

To a new beginning
Turn their faces
To my minstrelsongs
In this, the here and now

They press
To see my poem

Its
Orifices
Of ingress
Its ample intent

While
My flesh rots
And turns to moisture
Nightly rains will
Scatter

15.

The pure contralto sings in the organ loft
To the pilgrims and agnostics queuing up
To touch the sacred rock with the power
They say, to heal ailments: grippe; autism;
The body flux; mumps; shingles; sterility;
Tennis elbow; wrist, shoulder or Achilles
Tendinitis; lazy eye; leprosy; atrial flutter;
Tachycardia; pentosuria; benign essential
Tremor; renal calculi; Mad Cow Disease;
Tourette and Townes-Brocks syndrome;
Hyperglycemia; gangrene and cherubism.
The prayer or the hope of all is the same:
Heal me, clean me, make me whole. Not
The way the operating block does, where
What is removed drops horribly in a pail
Trimming to enforce
The myth of smoothness
That there is a form
That all forms strive
Towards
One
True
And immaculate.
The dream is other
To be both well and broken
To live and live fully in
The life
That our bodies
Allow us.

To be without weakness?
To be something less than dead.
The streets are full
Tonight, proud
Troops have returned
To their calm
Towns in Kansas
To a barely recognizable home
To Kentucky
To Iowa, to crowds that
Tell them they
Triumphed overseas
That now their long trek
Through the desert is over.
Miserable, muddleheaded you!
This is
Only the beginning of chaos.
To have killed
To have maimed, to have made
Another cease
This will not pass like delirious fever
It stays
Suppurates; it is
So. If the chaplain said
Otherwise
The chaplain lied. If the
Farmer speaks of the fields
Composting bone to humus
The poet of the graveyard yew
Pity them

It is abject
To count on the earth to redeem us
To ask time
To be
A balsam
And alchemical charm
A means to make beauty of grief

16.

I'm all over the place
Restless
My country a prison;
Sometimes it seems the
Only means to make
Anything one undertakes arrive
At anything much
And not emerge stillborn
Are shameful; the
Adoring hundred
Attending
A book launch
Come for the nibbles
Chat
And depart;
Across town it's
Opening night, an
Angry younger
Playwright

Is mocking society
Beautiful people
Amble in, and take

Their time
To take
Their place

17.

There I go again, typical me;
I accept nothing
If it is not perfect and nothing
Is perfect so I accept nothing

This is
Typical me

18.

What is
Important is not art's

Holy aura, Rufo, but how it funnels immensity
Into a simple person

Introducing the vast into the good enough and
Interim

Viewed thus good
Art is not the stuff we make a brouhaha
About (or don't) but a kind of dense lacuna:
A space that accepts
As much as it can contain

19.

The flower
Is ill
It is flimsy
Through having sucked
Toxins from the land
That
The weather
Turning
Turned infertile;
The gibbous moon

Drupelike
Widens

Draining the sun of its warmth
Do not, my friends
Deny

The little
I ask of you

20.

White wine
Hangover—gas and vomit

What about you

Are your own
Emissions unreasonable

Immense? Mine are, they cover
The planet like a cloud of sour breath

Westward
I see them and also to the East

Wrapped around the mountains

Hung upon the tree
Insinuating themselves

Into the lungs
And liver and jism

In each man's blood
They flow
And digress

I give off my particles
Infinitely; like a slew of stars
In the winter night

I send them out
If you need
I will belch some
Into your face or give you blessing from my bowel

I is not enough!
I must burst
And share my content

Offering myself
As
Indiscriminately as the dust

Motes in sunlight; as creeping fire
In
A slumbering house

21.

Interior, residual
The voice
That troubles me wakes me

I eat and eat and still stay thin
And in the night the floorboards moan
An

Interstitial living noise
Which
Is to me my cradle song and torment

How much will you put
In

It
Implores, what

Purpose this bottomless gut?
None I know of, I guess.
So stop. I can't.

Sleepy, I cross the hall to wash.
Endless. It is
Endless the impetus to get.
Endless the struggle to have.
Endless too the letting go forever.
Explain me that, voice!
Figure me how much
Sausage meat it takes

Precisely to stuff a courgette
Or chayote

22.

Yesterday's sun
Is
Inherent in the christophene
What can I possibly add?
Cilantro and borage
Dandelion and yuzu

Sunlight's
Subjects
Sunlight's lovely things
Her time-and-again bravura;
I contribute nothing, dice and toss

Phytoplankton
Exist and hence the bivalves

I though am distant, so almost incidentally
Stood in this room

It is as if I am not am but also

Wide
Eyed meercats peer at
Me from the TV set
I stare at them back and take them in

Documentary
Dripfeed

If you are with me
So far stay with me one more evening please
The place I am at

Tonight augurs madness
The window

Will shiver
The vacancy press against the bedroom wall

23.

Eggs
And coffee, and the pointilliste

Artillery of sparrows
Has chivvied February

Into April
Tits trill

It is a fecund, uncut
Morning

Hefty and fun
Folkloric
There are masques
There are maypoles
There is every human

Going-on that joins in and is
Yule giving
Into Spring

Life's
A shitty, thin
Affair without
A dash of the manic depressive

24.

Without, that is, imagination
To see and double the Spring
Now I am
Naked again, omnipotent

Underwriting each thing's
Unlikely thisness

With my own appropriate
Artistry; once

Taciturn, now prolix

I guarantee reality—
Blossoms

Turn to mushroom clouds
Vessels into boundless
Vistas
Various, drunken
And of
A piece, an afternoon
Of lager, angel dust and
Fog

This
Vision will
Vanish, they all do, but I passed

It to you, and that is much
It is much that I have made it
Correspond through my own gratuitous

Intellect and fists
Superimposing creation onto nature

Do you find I am
Too full of myself? Perhaps. But better
This

I say than what
The others would have you
Swallow; I need you
Follow you
Wake with you
Yet am not there
Beside you
My heartbeats
Rouse you
My appetite makes you
Thirst, I move in you
Sicken you
Vex and exhaust you
Yet despite this you
Welcome me, you
Build me up, you
Hold me long enough in you

It is
Empty
In the church
Now, the organ

That mesmerized plays no more
And the candles

The tourists lit cede to dark
The overdose smiles
To himself on the staircase

His body still, his breathing
Slow

Spring's publicity, winter's
Secret heaven

To have seen
The edge of paradise and
Then just disappear

25.

Do you remember the garden square
In which we slept one day in June

When
We woke in the dusk

My mouth
Was

Sure of itself
It knew the melody
Which the wood pigeon

Cooed, the way in which pollen
Drugs with its spread

We headed out
The world before us
Into the city's twilit
Miasma, and into a nameless
History

My dream
Escaping into London's noise;
I let it go and clung to you

We were lost in the
Infinite
Weekend public

26.

Now and then I can still hear the train
Transporting invisible freight

It is
Its own lodestone
Its own becoming
Sufficient
To itself, it rolls
Through the work-week
To nowhere;
Two parallel tracks
That never touch determine where it goes
Two parallel tracks
That never touch impel a cargo
Towards a station

I sit
In the outhouse and listen to the train's
Indifferent

Incantatory mantra
And find myself at ease

Anything repeated often enough is true:
The drip drip of ritual

Inches
The stalactites
Into form
Imperceptibly salts
Incrust to make girth
Slow falling water creates its own length
And obsession makes
Absence a thing

27.

After all, a form can form
Around pretty much anything:
The oyster shell a product of the pearl

Or take this ridged and calloused dome
It comes from me but is
Its own object also

I feel it on my palm
When I touch my palms together

28.

Incrementally
Future states
Transform
Me, as if
Only what is
Still to develop
Belongs: an inverse estoppel
Drawn out in time;
Unless the light
Dims
I will carry
This out (I have
No choice) forever
Fumbling to come
To that which preempts me

The egg-white
The feather
The crescent meringue

It is
Incipient in your
Idea of it; unmade

Yet not for that
Unununderstandable

29.

Bookish
Drunk, part-time

Philosopher, neurotic and modern
Requires maid

Sexual partner and occasional
Librarian

30.

Asymptotic symbiosis
That sees us start
The day off off and end it all but on;
This for years was the body's story
While the rest of our lives mapped another graph

Little by little
Tending apart until

One was too
Out on a limb to

Ascertain
If the other was
Around; then
After that, it was over
And what had seemed absolute, seemed ad hoc
And what was true, a chasm

31.

Icelandic moss
And gelatin
And miles of blinding asphalt;
A woman
A woman, a man and a boy
And over there
A line of gannets

In another lifetime, perhaps
Another time of year
And the tongues
Bloodied and the eyes put out

In angry minutes
In a frosted ditch
In the fungible shadow's
Impish collusions
In the calm of mildew
In heavenly snatch, in leafy
Ivy's
Intricate mess
Inscape and up and over
Itself

32.

In an emptying land
In a snow-kissed gulag

There where the fat man
Treads my boards
There where the hanged
Nymphs
Naked taunt me; to
Never be named, to never draw breath

Slow and hate-filled like the golem
Tripping contemptuous through the dawn

In death's
Delivery, its unpacking spasm

Mother
Grew me in her funny
Insides; a prism
Narrows the me from the millions
Pares

And perfects me for what if not for this?
Here is
Liveliness, here our land;
Evening

Holds me uncertain in its arm
Holds me uncertain

In
Warm
Emperilled adieu

33.

Spit it out,
Whatever it is,
Whatever the word
And its outlying

Myriad of things,
Incertitudes and suggestions
Is, will happen.

Bleached austral dawn
And a hundred
White impassible sailors
Piss and shave,
Shoreleave's brief horror
Washed away forever;
When the skittish
Wind grips you
With its carnival
Order or unbid
Obscurity newly descends,
Odors of silex,
Of liminal cunt;
Or when the
Spider on its
Web of breath
Waits all night
While humans talk
With millennial sorrow,
Wattles akimbo, jowls

Wet and glabrous,
Wiping their brows
With cow-flecked fingers,
Weak for bullion,
Weak for gold,
Weak for that
Which makes believe,
Which makes whatever
Was changeable less;
When the bow
Wastes and breaks
And the hard
Unlovely virgins cede,
Undone the decade,
Undone their refusal,
A blank-eyed skipper
And his crew
Are ballast and
Antipodes to this
Weird, unsettling mess.
What is normal
Weather anyway, given
Where the seasons
Went? Within the
Withered, dystopic bower
Where the sprawling
Weeds grow bullish,
Water alone is
Wealth, water without
Which our money

Worthless swells, determines
Whatever intrinsically counts.
We cannot own
What is unequal
To our eyes
That are themselves
Twinned damp collateral,
Pearls of fluid
Puzzling out the
Pulsing world's liquidity,
Parts of each
Person's better imagining
Leaching into us
Whenever we touch,
Making each essence
Convergent with many,
Flophouse of contact,
Brothel of heart,
Nodes where the
Vagabond others merge
Heaped in community,
Herded in dream,
Slotted together like
Wisdom on the
Shelf, like mind's
Synchronic and curious
Synapse, or that
Carcass of poultry
Simmered and blending,
Bouillon of vanishing
Inputs and stocks.

It is not
An agreeable hymn

I sing, atonal
Music, heavy words

In stiffly contrapuntal
Nets of time

If this simultaneity
Makes you puke

I couldn't care

If this book
Is panned that
Won't matter much
To me; only
Thing that matters
Terribly is idiom
Which meets and
Wrangles with an
Overwritten dense polysemy
To rejig language

It is autochthonous,
Inspired, full of
Ideas, of bollocks

My pecker is
Tetchy, the salad

Impeccable, in Minneapolis
The summer roses
Huddle and bloom.
Ho, ho, whores
And bless you
Happy festive clap;
Hope is just
Hunger dressed as
Holy lamb—abstention
And patience, trite
Impotent crap; appetite

Torments and exists
To be outrun,
To pray that
The longed-for desserts
Arrive is hokum

If the biscuits
Have no leaven
It needn't mean
It is mass.
The weeks reiterate,
The gathering empties

Align like schoolboys
In my kitchen,
More makes more

I stay unshaven
The shadow turns
Hairy, the bristles
Into beard, effortless
Terrible, fair enough

Is it appetite
Pushing these fleecy
Wires, or is
There something previous

Defining the shape
That appetite itself

Inhabits, coaxing lust
Into its million

Apparitions, inclining us
All towards Ens?
Are all the

Instances of life
Taken together unanimous;
The same shop
Where she gets
The baby lotion
They have another

Aisle that's stacked
High with dildos

34.

Never has so much
Impinged upon so
Nervous a crescendo;
The undone and the unsaid too
The thought thought and forgotten

Rawness
Nudity, primitive
Timbre
The tremor

That from nothingness
Makes it up
Lazily spews its narrative
Because, because it can it does;
Nine

Toadstools on a stump concur
Twelve pimples on a throat

Not at all
Sorry, in fact
And not at all clever
These things are
Simply
Themselves
And sit out their time, laying claim
To nothing beyond

A piece of sky that corresponds
To their own discrete dimension

35.

Waking turgid, skewy, perfect
With gaping mouth and profligate limbs
Light from the

Outside overlays me.
How many ways we lie
As we tickle ourselves

With what the thunder said;
Most books are worthless

Written by bums, or by a professor
Only the ones that are better than food

Fire me up, the rest are wank.
The things I said
That hurt you, I guess

They were lies
Too. Or else the kind of truth that

Only autists value
Truth uncut and absolute, and smaller
In meaning than a well-meant lie

Now that the sun
Which woke me is setting

Other suns will come
Other planets will kiss my sheet
There is

Too much down now for me to stop;
The stuff that stays unwritten

Never did excite me
To wait for daybreak is not to live

Once a thing

Set in motion
Halts allow
However long it takes

The show to restart and find its

36.

Sequel; and if it
Turns
Out to have stopped
Terminally, or that
Nearing completion
The author got the willies
Terrified of the hollow
Trough that greets any
Finished thing, tant pis—
Can't go crying over unmilked teats.
By the Sunday market
A rat is exploring
Darting around among the stalls
Tomorrow
When
The

37.

Yuppies
In the neighbourhood
Eat their daily biltong
Some will find hair in their muffin
And complain

Fuck such
Individuals that

Need to be
Insured against life's big mess

Need it be explained

Now we are knee-deep
My dear in this ongoing tract

A hair in a muffin is like hair on a bosom
Implying

38.

Enough is never enough.
Stop all this talk
Get going
If you want to make

The bus
The driver is
Temperamental, the night long

It will be a slow
Insomniac push across the plain; in
The bus
Crazies rock and simpletons chuckle

Incarcerated men
In jumpsuits
Ogle each
Tit and township as

Eagerly as wide-eyed
Children Christmas

39.

The
Itinerary is simple, straight

Into the expectant dawn
Iowa, Nebraska
Then veer towards L.A.

Where the scum
That wafts from Rotterdam

Beats and slaps against the
Shore; the bus proceeds
The convicts twitch, the dullards
Thumb their plastic gewgaws

40.

Further
You go

Emptier it gets
Salt, desert

Mountain, dirt;
A time back, at
Another poet's

Birthday
While I served myself

Yesterday's
Old ragù
Some poser with his
Idiotic wife
Arrived and saw

I was alone
You

Take a walk, he said, then
Offered me his
Arm

Over the grass
To the folly we went, over the waves

To colossal weather
To snow and blood
Lakes abhorrent and dense with phosphate

Ice on the lintel
On the thick
Black drainpipe

Ice on the sweltering compost heap;
Each object's edge
Lies

Somewhere beyond where we think it
None knows so none can tell you
If island and shelf
Are one, or one and two

41.

It slopes
And then it curls up

Into an incline
Hoarding detritus
Into a wall

Maybe the policy I
Once again attempt is
There in the continent's over-reach
Landmass redrawn
Buttressed by its own penumbra.
In a field
Where
There
Are animals
There is
Always a fence
Delimiting the
Pasture from the parcel
Newly sown;
Limits
Make corn
The absence of limits loss
But somewhere between
There is
The
Synecdoche by
Which a person

Travelling through
Darkness is allowed
To feel his
Totality at his
Borders, his neighbour
Partial, asleep on the bus

42.

And
Means all

Comma, communion:
Coterminous
Nondescript, lived-in

Every time

My parrots squawk
My own
Falsetto finds equivalence

Emitted
Exogenous
Ephemeral
Expressions
Each
Effeminate
Eunuch

Hearing
Thing
Talking
Meaning
Agog

Tries
With all his
Throat to replicate

The first word is
Itself and others'
Inputs, language
Wrought from
Egg and sperm

I held my offspring, changed them
Knew them and their tastes
And sent them off

Near ready into life
Buying
Them time by
Trading our futures;
The kids will be kids
Impressed by us
They
Tend to other stuff
Something of their own
Apropos and disparate

43.

It lasts forever
Make no mistake, its
Endless contours unfolding within
Bounds.
Whenever I am weak in
Mind fractals
Haunt me with their paisley swags
Drawn without
Drawing or design
Worlds of slalom
And self-taught line
That follow
Routes of their own unnerve me
Laying down unwound
Behind my eyes

On the starchy

Daybed
Fitful
I drop off

Hand in crotch
High on Dilaudid

By your works
I shall know you, by
Their incarnate
Ambition and scope

If the work is good
Bugger life's upheaval

Early one evening with time to kill

I walked
Near the
New university, when
Night fell
Novel forms of surrender
Niggled me, infinity
Nothingness, girls in
Nylon tights; they slouch
Narcotic against my arm
Now, they say, about the canon

44.

I am fed up

With my
Imbecilic kin

They are

Watching the oceans
Turn to algal bloom

Bloody
Awful, they

Interject, their
Tongues all crusty

With the breakbone fever
I've never seen the like
And cultivate their garden;
When

It rains the

Motorfumes
Overwhelm us
And in the sunshine heat

Reeks on concrete.
A long time
I sat
Among the businessmen

Listening

Intently to the
Few who made sense

Clothed in
Fear they repeat themselves
The audience

Buy it but the
Markets don't

Flaccid web
Too big to discern
Vast and passive
Mute and late

Abstract, man-made
Noncommittal

45.

Our Spring, they
Opine, begins in April

Mine does not, it starts at any time
Creep of season
Jibing with my art
Commanding the land
Contracting it chemical into birth.
Like
Bees
Nurse and feed the

Obscene grub jelly, strangers

Endow me with their stuff
And fade away

Into the mass;
An orderly is

Wringing
Out the rancid

Mattress
Heavy with sweat
And cold cream

The
Impregnated cushion
Washed
And rinsed into the river

At
The first

Sign of life they bolt,
Curators in suits that

Mistaken
Take this
Text for true

46.

It is and

It isn't; it is all
Manner of things
Neither
In nor out of the ordinary.
If one
Beautiful
Morning we all went
Minnowing would

Names and dates still find you?
You slide yourself

Into the analyst's couch
Pound at the window
Plead with the dead

Sob in the darkness that nothing is enough;
Well nothing is but still the fish go

Infallibly curious into my trap—
A little
Fish, bait for a salmon

There is in
Anything handed on
A background

You
Intuit in the thing itself

Salmon
Herring, rock
Bass, hake

Lungfish digging in the drying shallows
Nightcrawlers
Yeast spores, the archaic microbe

Let them be—
Newer
Taxa will overturn the order

47.

I'm alright, this
Homework is fun
Harder draft awaits the teacher

That set the test
Which he will be forever
Forced to mark
Using up his
Foreign coins to
Play indefinitely at my slots.
An

Image
Is forming, an earlier
Minimum

Is all but fleshed out
Ingénu
Transformed

Into habitué;
A great-breasted dancer

Is moving around a pole
Turning slowly
Then in widening arcs

No-one even looks, the
Birthday

Table are drunk and pitiful
Tired by
The
Islanders and by their rum

The
Only person vaguely on form
Or faking it, is the

Man that
Takes admission;
The dancer circles to the
Tawdry music, the
Talcum moving through the club like blossom

48.

Initially
And after all
As if it was
A three-day weekend
An unfamiliar touch
Arranges
All the hullabaloo
And nudges it to sense
And it is

As if the order existed;
Father said
Nothing when I came home with

Impetigo, he just
Necked a glass of

Whiskey
Infection
Is
Inevitable
Among siblings, and playmates too
Over time, said the doctor

49.

After the

Tea and biscuits
I notice that the light is failing
It is
About five

And the
Iceshelf is calving
In the northern seas

At home and at a loss
Now I picture the

Iceberg fizz and groan;
Outside the curtains
It is snowing

On the orchard, a dust
Of snow that
Turns the dark
Trees

Into light
It falls on the ground
And on my windowsill

50.

The house

We are renting has
Its own agenda, moving

Inside it we are lived
In too, ancestral

Symbols hang in
The

Privy, your face is

Daubed in likeness
In the music room upstairs

51.

The bedroom
Appalls me

Look at the
Lady fingering
The lodger

Down the hall the shelf
Voids itself
It pours

Its salts into the bathtub

Whatever
We purchase

Winds up here

52.

The iron bath is filling

It is a museum piece
Impractical, fit to be conserved

The man whose smithy made
It's dying for a piss;
In the vapor and murk

I see his white apron
Inch up his fleshy thighs

It is so dirty, the
Image looks bereft of focus

Yet we know the man
By his good blue eyes
And by your own sad

Fears that a first word
May be one and over;
I stop waiting for you

Photo by Renaud Monfourny

Rufo Quintavalle was born in London in 1978, studied at Oxford and the University of Iowa and lives in Paris. He is the author of numerous books of poetry including *hhereenow*, *Weather Derivatives*, *Dog, cock, ape and viper* and *Anyone for anymore*. He used to run the reading series, Poets Live, and for several years taught creative writing at NYU's Paris campus. He is co-creator and lead actor in an innovative film and poetry project called *Coldhearts: A Poetical*—it's a bit like a musical but with more poetry and fewer twirling umbrellas.

www.ingramcontent.com/pod-product-compliance
Lightning Source LLC
Chambersburg PA
CBHW031146090426
42738CB00008B/1245